Always and Forever

LARA LYS

A POETRY BOOK

To my Lilly,

In every verse, you are my muse.

My inspiration, my love.

Always and forever yours.

Always and forever mine.

CONTENTS

CONTENTS

Beneath the starry sky, I'd roam.
In your arms, I found my home.
Love from yesterday all but washed away.
When you graced my life in sweet array.
Like a fortress, my hearts defenses fell.
A treasure trove in you, I could tell.
Night by night, our love did brew.
Irresistible, my heart was drawn to yours.
To you.

Starry Embrace

Your love, a tale of endless grace.
In every moment, in every place.
A never ending story yours and mine.
In our love, forever we entwine.
But remember, before loving another's face,
love your own.
Find your embrace.

Self Symphony

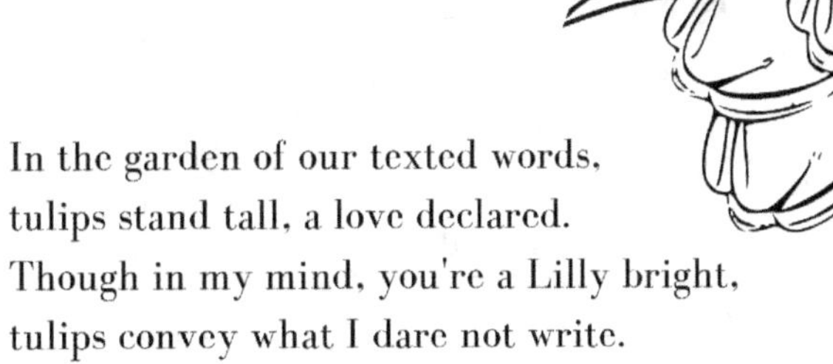

In the garden of our texted words,
tulips stand tall, a love declared.
Though in my mind, you're a Lilly bright,
tulips convey what I dare not write.

Beside your name, a tulip blooms,
symbolizing love's perfect tunes.
Each petal a whisper, each stem a plea,
to show you the love that envelops me.

Do you grasp why tulips appear?
In every message, every sincere tear?
They symbolize a love so deep.
In every embrace, its secrets keep.

With each message, a tulip's sent,
a token of love, a sweet lament,
For in every breath, in every sigh,
my love for you, it'll never die.

So, when you see those tulips bright,
know they carry my love, day and night.
In every bloom, in every hue.
Forever, my love, I give to you.

Blooming Messages

In love's cruel dance, a bitter play unfolds,
Where professed adoration turns cold.
Beneath the veneer of affection's veil,
Lies betrayal's sting, like a venomous snail.

Discovery dawns, a tempestuous morn,
As lies unravel, trust is torn.
The soul, afflicted, with anguish untold,
A sickness festers, a tale yet untold.

Like quaking earth 'neath thunderous skies,
Faith crumbles, illusions guise.
Idols of devotion, now fractured, frayed,
In falsehood's grip, our hearts are swayed.

Betrayal's blade, a wound profound,
Leaving us raw, our spirits bound.
Yet they return, with contrite pleas,
Seeking solace, on bended knees.

Words, mere echoes, in the hollow night,
Deception's cloak, veiling contrite.
Each apology, a shallow grave,
For the trust they buried, a heart to save.

No salve exists for wounds so deep,
Where secrets fester, shadows creep.
In the end, a crossroad's sight,
To cling to darkness or embrace the light.

A Ballad Of Betrayal

Wanting you, the sweetest song I'd pursue.
 When you entered my life, and love grew.
Once again my walls they crumbled down,
in your presence and priceless self.
Night by night our love anew
My heart forever melted for you.

Melodies Of Love

In shadows dim, I pondered alone,
"I don't think she loves me anymore."
Echoes of doubt, like a mournful tone,
And I, too, shun the one I bore.

For in comfort's embrace, I transform,
Into a specter, a dreadful sight.
Haunted by whispers, a lingering storm,
Am I the cause of their quiet flight?

Truth's elusive veil veils my sight,
"If that's the truth or not, I'll never know."
In the depths of uncertainty's night,
My thoughts, the only truth I sow.

Within my mind, a sanctuary true,
Where honesty reigns, unwaveringly so.
In solitude's embrace, I rue,
"I think," the only solace and hell I know.

U n c e r t a i n r y

In shadows cast by doubt's embrace,
Whispers haunt in silent space,
Sometimes, just sometimes, I fear,
Your hidden thoughts, not made clear.

When names of friends slip past my ear,
And hours vanish, your path unclear,
Do you shield me from eyes to see?
Sometimes, just sometimes, embarrassed of me?

Your words, once soft, now rigidly bend,
"I'm just a friend," a hollow blend.
My touch, once welcomed, now denied,
Do you hide me, casting love aside?

In vagueness veiled, your life's tableau,
A canvas painted with shadows to grow.
Do you fear what light may reveal,
Sometimes, just sometimes, embarrassed to feel?

But if you knew the weight I bear,
Would love's gentle warmth repair?
Would walls of doubt and fear unlace,
In the sanctuary of love's embrace?

So let your heart unfurl and soar,
In love's embrace, forevermore.
For in this bond, so true and free,
Embarrassment finds no decree.

.

S h a d o w s   O f   F e a r

Your love a saga, endless and divine.
in every moment our souls entwine.
A never ending story, yours and mine.
In this love, forever we'll shine.
With you my love, an eternal sign.
In this never-ending story, you are mine.

Timeless Bond

In dreams I find your gentle grace,
A smile upon my lips, your embrace.
Through whispered words and tender gaze,
In every moment, love's song plays.

With each heartbeat, a dance ensues,
A rhythm formed by love's sweet muse.
Seventy-two, a count so true,
Yet none as precious as when with you.

In every pause, love's tale is spun,
Two beats skipped, lost in the run.
For in my heart, a symphony so grand,
Love's melody, eternally planned.

"I love you" echoes, soft and clear,
Yet deeper still, you're ever near.
In every breath, in all I do,
Love resides, forever in you.

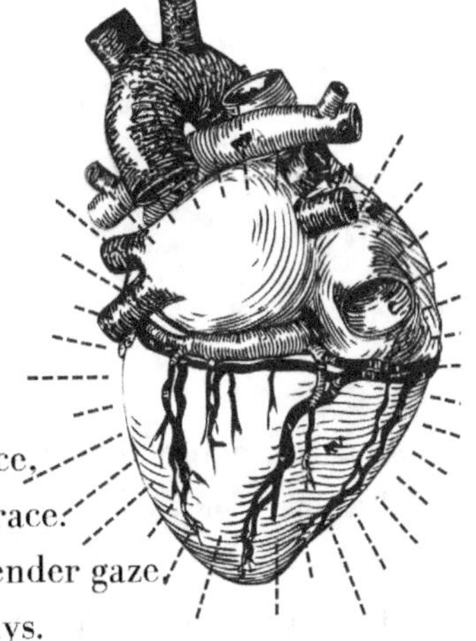

B e a t s   F o r   Y o u

In the quiet moments, when candles gleam,
I wished for you, my silent dream.
For your happiness, in every way,
For our love to flourish, day by day.

I wished for safety, for you and me,
In the embrace of love's harmony.
For health to grace us, in every breath,
For our souls to dance, in love's sweet depth.

And as I blew out the candles, one by one,
I wished for love, to forever run.
For eternity to embrace our souls,
In love's embrace, where destiny unfolds.

My Birthday Wish

In silence, a void, a pause unfurls,
883 days, a constant whirl.
No morning whispers, no words so sweet,
A break in the rhythm, a silent retreat.

No cute calls, no dreams to share,
Just empty spaces, lingering in the air.
No questions asked, no longing confessed,
In the absence of us, a moment to digest.

Is this the path to healing, to mend the heart?
To untangle the threads, to find a fresh start?
In the quiet absence, a question looms near,
Is this what healing is, when love disappears?

Abscense Of You

Caught between longing and letting go,
In a moment's breath, I found my woe.
Waiting for you, yet craving to erase,
Two conflicting desires, in the same space.

To linger in hope or to bid farewell,
In this dilemma, I could not quell.
So I found myself, in a strange ballet,
Waiting and forgetting, night and day.

Yearning for your presence, yet craving release,
A paradoxical dance, a restless peace.
Stuck between two worlds, uncertain and sublime,
In the limbo of longing, lost in time.

My Dilemma

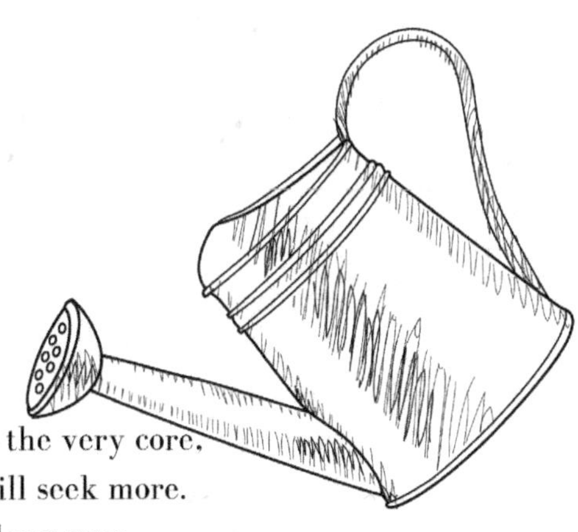

For you, I'd change the very core,
Sacrifice all, and still seek more.
In your light, I find my way,
With every step, a debt to pay.

You're the seed for growth, the reason I strive,
In your presence, I feel alive.
Every effort, every ache, every hue,
All worth it, for the chance to be with you.

You're worth it all, I implore,
Just see your worth, let it soar.

The Things I Would Do

If you'd permit, I'd liken you to the sky,
Gather your flaws, weave them into a celestial tie.
In your doubts, I'd find beauty to adore,
Each imperfection, a star to explore.

You dispute when called beautiful, I see,
Yet, what you loathe, I cherish endlessly.
With your consent, I'd craft an observatory grand,
To reveal your radiance, across the vast expanse spanned.

For all the stars in the cosmos, in their celestial queue,
None outshine the brilliance, none as bright as you.

All Your Flaws

In her embrace, I found true love's embrace,
Not fleeting, not feigned, but genuine grace.
Real and raw, her love did shine,
A beacon of purity, a love divine.

Kindness flowed in every deed,
In her love, I found all I need.
Filled with truth, it set me free,
Her love, a balm that healed me.

She showed me love, in every way,
No falsehoods, no shadows, just light of day.
No hate, no anger, in her tender care,
She loved me wholly, beyond compare.

For who I am, she loved me true,
And in her love, I learned to renew.
To love myself, as she does so pure,
With every beat, my love for her endures.

In Your Love

In love's grand dance, I take my stand,
No room for whispers, only grand,
For if my love can't reach the sky,
It fades away, a silent sigh.
So know this truth, both clear and tall,
If I can't love you vast, my heart will fall.

Love's Dance

Once, your words weighed heavy, laden with sorrow,
Of dreams shattered, of uncertain tomorrows.
She spoke of another, of vows to be spoken,
While your heart, aching, silently broken.

In our love's embrace, I dreamed of us,
Of weddings and children, no thoughts of fuss.
Calling you my wife, our forever so true,
Yet now, my dreams lie shattered, no longer in view.

You once shared my dreams, our spirits intertwined,
But now, you've turned away, leaving love behind.
To walk a different road, with another by your side,
Leaving me to mourn, in love's bitter tide.

No more can I dream, of love's sweet refrain,
Of laughter and joy, family and love, washed away in pain.
My heart lies shattered, in the depths of despair,
As love's fading ember leaves me bare.

Dreams To Ashes

In the gentle caress of love's tender embrace,
I yearn for baths drawn, with petals in place.
To feel your hands, gentle upon my hair,
As you wash away worries, with love and care.

Endless kisses, like whispers of the breeze,
Soft hugs, like blankets, bringing ease.
Your warm smile, a beacon in the night,
Guiding me home, in love's soft light.

To listen, to truly hear, with heart wide open,
Holding hands, fingers interwoven.
Your thumb tracing patterns, on my skin so fine,
A silent promise, of love intertwined.

To meet your gaze, lost in your eyes' deep sea,
As you move my hair, declaring me free.
In your tender touch, I find solace, pure and true,
In this soft, gentle love, I find my sanctuary with you.

My Sanctuary

As dawn's gentle fingers caress the sky,
The hardest moment draws nigh.
From slumber's embrace, I slowly part,
But waking to your absence shatters my heart.

In the hushed whispers of night's embrace,
Illusions weave, dreams softly trace.
Yet with morning's light, reality's cruel art,
Reveals the void, tearing me apart.

Sleep's tender promises, a fleeting dance,
But with each sunrise, grief's cruel lance.
Every morning, the truth etched deep,
You're gone, and the pain does not sleep.

Mourning You

In every word, a whisper of devotion,
Each phrase a pledge, a heartfelt notion.
With every breath, I strive to convey,
My love for you, in every way.

Are you hungry, my heart
I love you, in every part.
Look at the sun, its gentle glow,
I love you more than you'll ever know.

In the tapestry of time, our love weaves,
In every moment, it quietly cleaves.
So hear my words, sincere and true,
I love you, always and forever, I do.

My Heart

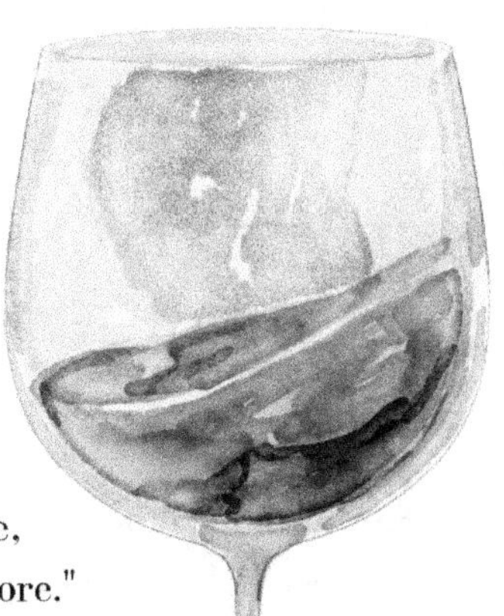

In shadows dim, I pondered alone,
"I don't think she loves me anymore."
Echoes of doubt, like a mournful tone,
And I, too, shun the one I bore.

For in comfort's embrace, I transform,
Into a specter, a dreadful sight.
Haunted by whispers, a lingering storm,
Am I the cause of their quiet flight?

Truth's elusive veil veils my sight,
"If that's the truth or not, I'll never know."
In the depths of uncertainty's night,
My thoughts, the only truth I sow.

Within my mind, a sanctuary true,
Where honesty reigns, unwaveringly so.
In solitude's embrace, I rue,
"I think," the only solace and hell I know.

U n c e r t a i n r y

Smile for me, a tender grace,
That whispers love in a timeless embrace.
For in your smile, my inner child finds peace,
A love that soothes, a joy to release.

Laugh for me, like melodies divine,
A symphony of joy, like aged wine.
Your laughter, a thrill, a rush so sweet,
In its echo, my heart finds complete.

Hold me close, in your tender embrace,
A sanctuary of love, a sacred space.
For in your touch, I find my crown,
A treasure beyond all renown.

Look at me, with eyes so true,
In their depths, I find my view.
For without your gaze, plain to see,
I'm but a shadow, lost at sea.

So smile, laugh, hold, and look at me,
In your love, I find my eternity.

For Me

In the quiet spaces between us, I knew,
This inevitable unraveling, this truth.
From subtle shifts in glances, in tone,
I sensed the change, felt it in my bones.

Your responses, once warm, now cold,
The weight of unspoken words took hold.
With each passing moment, a silent fear,
Yet I dared not voice, lest it draw near.

Perhaps, I thought, I'm merely lost in thought,
But deep down, uncertainty wrought.
And when the words finally found their way,
Confirming my fears, in disarray.

You echoed thoughts I dared not say,
And in that moment, pain held sway.
To be right, yet to ache so deep,
In this bittersweet truth, secrets keep.

So I knew, long before it came to be,
That this rift between us, I'd soon see.
For in the silence, in the subtle signs,
Lies the truth, painful yet divine.

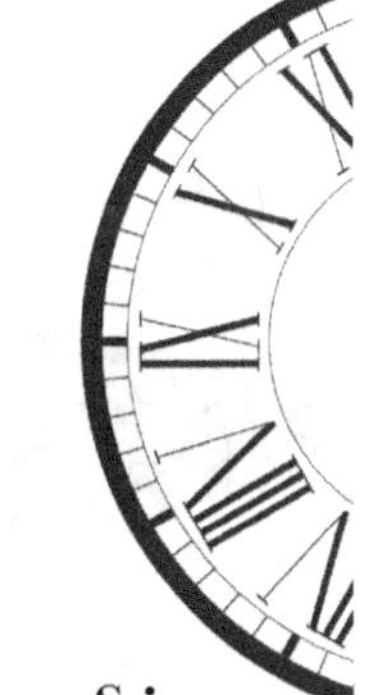

Your Subtle Signs

These words, an anchor in my chest they rest,
Heavier than water, weighing down my breast.
If upon the coldest seas, I lay adrift,
Beneath the waves, my sorrow, a silent rift.

No buoyancy in this ocean of despair,
As grief pulls me down, unaware.
In the depths, where shadows loom,
I sink, consumed by sorrow's gloom.

For every syllable, a weight to bear,
Dragging me deeper, with every prayer.
Tethered to this anguish, I descend,
Where solace eludes, and sorrows blend.

In Your Distance

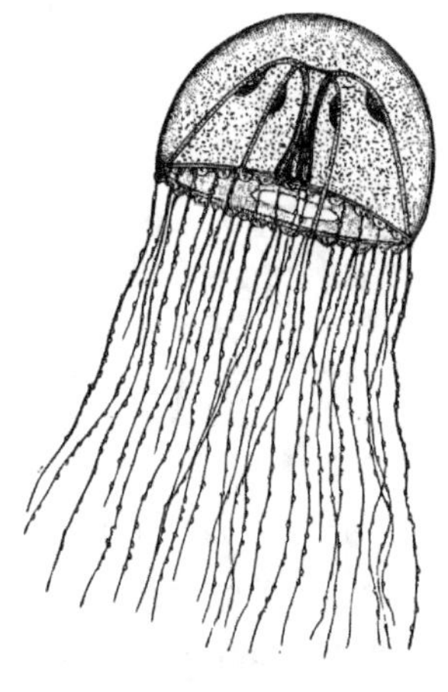

Every part of me, a silent plea,
Yearning for love, desperately.
Yet deep within, a child cries,
"I fear I'm unlovable," she sighs.

"Do you ever think," I softly ask,
"That love for me could ever last?"
A question posed, with hope entwined,
Seeking solace for the heart's confined.

Likes and longing, in whispers spun,
Hoping for love beneath the sun.
Yet amidst the echoes of desire's plea,
Lies a soul, longing to be free.

What You Left Behind

"My lilly," I murmur, soft and clear,
In your embrace, I find solace near.
Never doubt, in this journey untold,
Your place in my soul, forever holds.

You'll never know a love less true,
For you're woven in every hue.
In the tapestry of my very being,
Your essence, my heart's decreeing.

So rest assured, in this endless scroll,
Your name, forever my heart's parole.
Bound by love's unbreakable seal,
My darling, your love, I eternally feel.

My Lilly

In the shadows, I've mastered the art,
Of hiding the cracks within my heart.
Pretending I'm okay, though it's a lie,
I've learned to smile, to laugh, to try.

But deep down, I know the truth,
That everything's not fine, despite my sleuth.
I fear it may never be as before,
Yet I paint a facade, a mask I wore.

With every smile, every laugh, every gleam,
I radiate enough, or so it seems.
People admire, they see what they want to see,
Not knowing it's all for them, just for thee.

My Facade

Before you, selflessness adorned my soul's attire,
Yet in your presence, selfishness sets fire
Oh, how my heart succumbs to this desire,
To claim you wholly, stoke love's blazing pyre.

Selfishly I yearn, a possessive flame,
To be your sole keeper, in love's game.
I crave your touch, your lips, your embrace,
In this selfish love, I find my place.

For no other arms shall hold you tight,
No other lips shall taste your delight.
I am selfish, unabashedly so,
In my love for you, this I gladly show.

Call me selfish, let the echoes ring,
For in my selfish love, I spread my wing.
For you, my darling, I'll proudly declare,
In this selfish love, I'll tenderly ensnare.

N o   O n e   E l s e

In the shadows where your secrets reside,
Tell me, love, where do you hide?
Which part of yourself do you shun the most,
So I may know where my lips should boast?

Sweetness in heart, yet soul stained with ink,
You needn't pretend, let your truths sink.
In your flaws and scars, I find my home,
For in your darkness, my love will roam.

What You Hide

In every part of you, my heart found delight,
From your smile so radiant, to laughter's flight.
Those eyes, a window to a soul so true,
With humor and passion, my love for you grew.

How could I not, when you embody my dreams,
Every facet of you, in love's gentle streams.
You're all I've ever craved, my heart's truest call,
In loving you wholly, I've given my all.

H o w   C o u l d   I   N o t   L o v e   Y o u

In the stillness of my childhood room, she sat,
A younger echo, a mirror of my past, so intact.
Seven years old, on my bed, she lingered there,
Lost, with innocence veiled by a cloud of despair.

Approaching her gently, I knelt down to her side,
Taking her tiny hands, where sadness did reside.
Her voice, fragile, echoed in the room's quiet,
"Where's mommy? I miss her," her words, a silent riot.

With a heavy heart, I whispered, "She won't return."
Her eyes welled with tears, her small soul did yearn.
"Never?" she questioned, hope flickering dim,
"Not for a long while," I admitted, heart brimming.

As tears flowed freely, I held her close, so small,
Her face in my hands, a moment to recall.
"Does she not love us?" her broken voice inquired,
My own smile fading, my composure tired.

"I don't know," I confessed, uncertainty stark,
Her gaze, shattered, pierced through the dark.
"Are we unlovable?" her voice trembled in pain,
My facade crumbling, her innocence waning.

"I don't know," I repeated, truth ringing clear,
Then, like a whisper, she vanished, disappeared.
Gone, yet her echo lingers, haunting my soul,
A reminder of love's absence, an unending toll.

The Pieces You Destroyed

In every beat of my heart, I hold true,
Your faith in me, a steadfast view.
With every fiber, your belief takes flight,
In me and my dreams, your trust alight.

Your words, a melody, echo clear,
A constant reminder, always near.
As my journey unfolds, you're by my side,
My soundboard, my supporter, my pride.

With your cheer, I rise above,
In your belief, I find endless love
Unstoppable, with you as my guide,
Forever in your trust, I confide.

Believe In Me, Believe In You

In life's journey, some souls we meet,
Who bring a calmness, pure and sweet.
They breathe new life into our days,
With every word, in subtle ways.

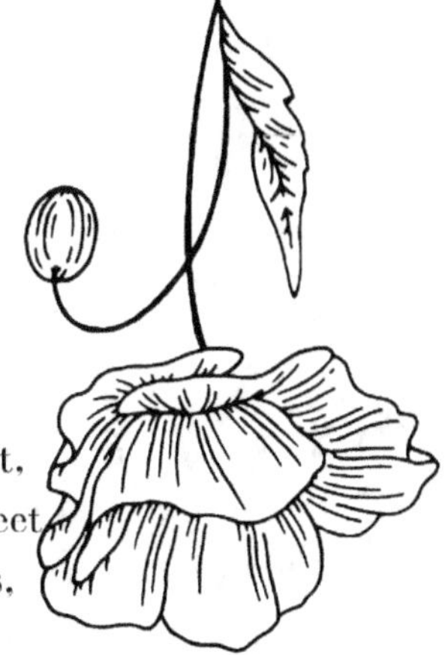

Encouraging dreams, with hearts so kind,
No jealousy, just love entwined.
Their joy in our victories, sincere and true,
In their presence, the world feels anew.

Warmth and brightness, in their gaze,
Love and loyalty, in endless praise.
With them, happiness blooms like a flower,
In their embrace, we find our power.

Authentically happy, in their glow,
The best version of ourselves, they show.
For those rare souls, we're forever grateful,
In their love and light, our hearts feel full.

Your Warmth, Your Gaze

In the quiet of whispered vows,
"I love you more," my heart avows.
Not a tally of affection's store,
But a pledge to endure, to explore.

Beyond the shadows of days to come,
Beyond the battles we may succumb,
My love for you, a steadfast shore,
In every tempest, forevermore.

Across the expanse where distance resides,
My love for you, it never hides.
It transcends the barriers, the walls we erect,
In its embrace, all doubts deflect.

So when I profess, "I love you the most,"
It's a symphony, a heartfelt boast.
In the tapestry of our love's sweet toast,
You're the melody, the eternal host.

I love You More

Sleep escapes me, thoughts of you invade,
Your voice echoes, in the quiet cascade.
Tossing, turning, in the midnight haze,
I clutch my pillow, lost in your gaze.

By the window, I seek the night's embrace,
I draw back the curtains, to be in the stars' grace.
A celestial choir,
Whispering softly, igniting desire.

"Don't worry," they murmur, "love's gentle dove,"
In their little dance, a message of love.
With stars as my witness, I find solace there,
In the quiet of night, love fills the air.

W h i s p e r s   O f   L o v e

In the silence of your absence, echoes ring,
Louder than words, your silence stings.
My tears break the stillness, a torrential flow,
"I love you," whispered, in the undertow.

Against reason's counsel, I dare to speak,
"I LOVE YOU," the words leak.
Hours crawl, a slow-paced waltz of despair,
Lies swarm in the void, a heavy air.

My heart, once whole, now fractures anew,
From you, this heartache, unexpected, true.
In the shattered fragments, your memory weaves,
A tapestry of longing, where my soul grieves.

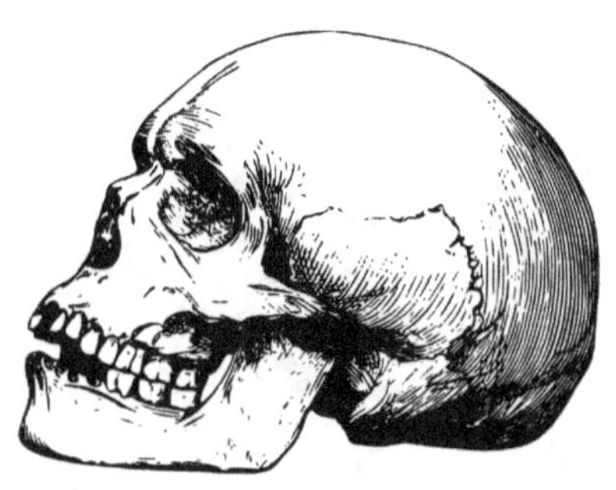

My Grieving Soul

In silent gazes, secrets bloom,
Shared smiles across a crowded room.
A touch, a laugh, a whispered phrase,
Love's language in fleeting days.

"I heard this song," a whispered line,
A moment shared, hearts entwine.
Comfort found in quiet grace,
In each other's warm embrace.

Apologies spoken, forgiveness found,
In tender moments, love's profound.
Trust and laughter, hand in hand,
In every gesture, love's command.

"You're my love," a cherished vow,
In deepest trust, we take our bow.
Crying alone, yet not apart,
In shared tears, love restarts.

Heart-to-heart, in whispers true,
In understanding, love renews.
A final kiss, a gentle sigh,
In parting's touch, love still lies.

A sense of safety, a feeling known,
In love's embrace, we are home.
Believing in love's steadfast sway,
In every moment, come what may.

You In My Mind

In the dance of hands, a silent art,
Fingers entwine, never to part.
How effortlessly they find their place,
In the tender grasp of love's embrace.

In the warmth of arms, a sacred space,
Where hearts find solace, find their grace.
Cheek to neck, in perfect alignment,
A sanctuary found in love's refinement.

It's no mere chance, this symphony,
Of bodies entwined, in unity.
Designed to love, to hold, to share,
In every breath, in every prayer.

For in the weave of flesh and bone,
Love finds its dwelling, its eternal throne.
A testament to our divine decree,
That in each other, we find our key.

Our Silent Art

In your absence, I yearn for more,
For sunny skies and storms that roar.
For laughter shared and tears we shed,
For all the things, both loved and dread.

I ache for moments lost in time,
For every peak and every climb.
I long to feel your presence near,
To hold you close and quell my fear.

Though you're gone, your essence stays,
In memories, in heartfelt praise.
I crave the fullness of your being,
In every joy and every seeing.

So come back to me, in sun or rain,
In laughter's joy or sorrow's pain.
For with you, I find my all,
In every rise and every fall.

Your Essence

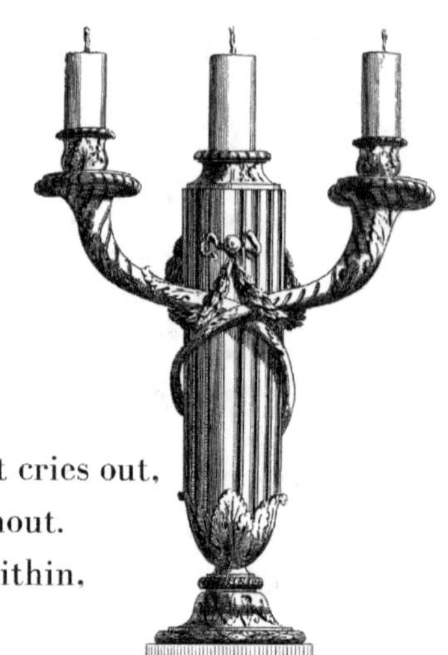

In the depths of night, my heart cries out,
Longing to tear, to scream, to shout.
To rend my chest, and search within,
For every shard of love and sin.

With trembling hands, I'd grasp each piece,
To make you feel, the pain's increase.
But love holds fast, its gentle sway,
Restrains my fury, day by day.

Though your mistakes, like daggers gleam,
And shattered promises haunt my dreams.
I cannot yield to vengeance's call,
For love still lingers, after all.

So I carry on, with wounds so raw,
Bleeding from the scars you saw.
Each day a struggle, to endure,
The sharp edges of love unsure.

Yet still, beneath the weight of pain,
A flicker of hope, remains.
That soon enough, you'll love me right.
So I'll wait for you, to make things right.

Love's Lament

Through the storms and through the calm,
In every trial, in every balm,
A whisper lingers, soft and clear,
Of a day when you'll again be near.

Not just a thought within my mind,
Not just a memory left behind,
But a reality, strong and true,
Where I can once again call you.

In the depths of night, that whisper stays,
Guiding me through endless days.
A beacon bright, a steady sign,
That soon, you'll be mine.

So I hold onto hope, in light and shade,
In every journey that we've made.
For I believe in love's sweet art,
And in the power of a hopeful heart.

Through It All

In the void of distance, where echoes fade to naught,
"You were so far away, my cries all for naught,"
"I tried every avenue, what else could I construe?"
With a choked sob, I plead, "Just love me,
Love me in whispers, devoid of guilt's cruel sting."

A tear-stained confession, a heart laid bare,
"Love me," I implore, a fervent prayer.
"You were meant to hold, to cherish, to see,"
In the tapestry of love, our souls seek to be free.

Just Love Me

In silent whispers, my heart speaks to you,
Unveiling thoughts hidden from view.
I wish you knew the depths within,
The feelings stirred when our eyes begin.

Each glance a symphony, each gaze a clue,
Echoing the sentiment, if only you knew.
In crowded spaces, amidst the throng,
I search for you, where I belong.

Direction altered, paths anew,
Simply to catch a glimpse of you.
I wish you knew, in whispers true,
My fondness grows, for you I pursue.

All We Knew

In the quiet of night, as stars softly gleam,
I battled sleep's grasp, in a desperate scheme.
To shield my heart from the ache of dreams,
Where your absence reigns in silent streams.

In the hush of darkness, where shadows play,
I clung to wakefulness, keeping sleep at bay.
For in the realm of dreams, you'd slip away,
Leaving me yearning at the break of day.

Each moment awake, a fragile reprieve,
From the sorrow that lurked in dreams' weave.
Yet even in solitude, your presence would bloom,
A bittersweet whisper in night's gentle gloom.

In My Dreams

In pursuit of happiness, I tread each day,
Yet time slips by, in an endless sway.
Two years vanish, leaving me adrift,
In depths unknown, my spirits sift.

Yearning for change, a futile quest,
Met with disappointment, an unwelcome guest.
Yet still I strive, to break the chain,
Even if it means embracing pain.

I'll grasp at any chance, however brief,
To find solace, to find relief.

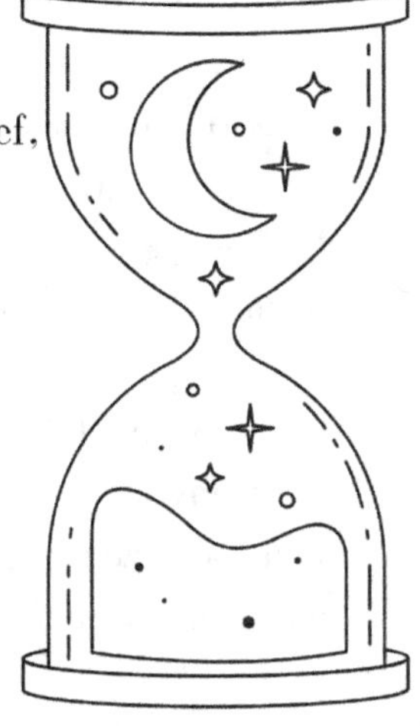

Two Years

In her eyes, a world unfurls,
A mesmerizing gaze, it swirls.
I'm drawn in deep, afraid yet thrilled,
By love's embrace, my heart fulfilled.

Your eyes, a portal to your soul,
Revealing truths beyond control.
With every glance, I'm lost in you,
A love so pure, so deeply true.

But in the depths of your soul's gaze,
I fear the truth my heart betrays.
For if you see the love I hide,
All words would fade, no need to bide.

Just two souls, locked in a trance,
Lost in love's sweet, silent dance.
So let me gaze into your eyes,
And drown in love's eternal ties.

Lost In Your Eyes

Loving you is akin to loving the sun,
Intensity ablaze, where passions run.
For love devoid of heat, a pale disguise,
In flames, we find the truth that never lies.

It's the fiery fervor that defines our bond,
A love untamed, fierce and fond.
Embracing the blaze, we dare to ignite,
For in its scorching glow, we find our light.

Our Fiery Love

Upon your sight, the game was done,
Life shifted course, a new begun.
Pink fades to blue, a hue so true,
Your laughter's charm, my favorite view.

Love, once hid, now boldly shown,
Embraced, in warmth, it's fully grown.
Alone no more, in your embrace,
Anxiety quelled, in your grace.

With intertwined hands, our story's told,
Life's canvas painted, rich and bold.
A single rose to blooms untold,
For your love, a beauty, manifold.

Pink To Blue

Navigating the pace, a delicate dance,
With shared toothbrushes, perhaps a chance.
Matching tattoos, a bond so true,
Exploring Paris, just me and you.

Cuddles and love, steps we take,
In this journey together, no need to forsake.
Though cautious we tread, our hearts entwine,
In the tender embrace of love's design.

.

A Delicate Dance

Your presence echoes in the chambers of my mind,
Each word, each moment, a treasure to find.
In the quiet spaces, where silence may dwell,
Know that your essence, no words can dispel.

Your impact lingers, in memories deep,
A cherished presence, in moments we keep.
Though silence may linger, know this to be true,
You're unforgettable, in all that you do.

Your Silence

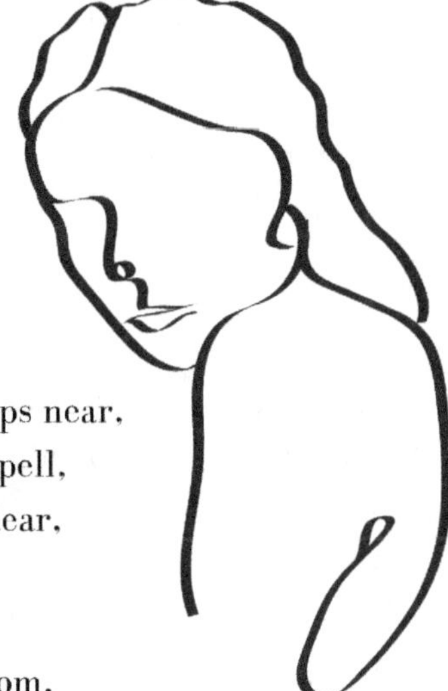

In the depths of night, fear creeps near,
A haunting thought, a chilling spell,
The thought of losing you, my dear,
A terror that I cannot quell.

For in your absence, shadows loom,
A void where once your presence dwelt,
To lose you is to face my doom,
A fate with which I cannot melt.

Yet even as the darkness grows,
And whispers echo in my mind,
I'd brave the depths, confront the woes,
To keep your light forever shined.

For in this world, amidst the strife,
Your love, a beacon, guides me through,
The thought of losing you, my life,
Is scarier than losing myself, it's true.

Losing Me, or Losing You

In the dance of life, I sway with grace,
Sensitive soul, attuned to each trace,
A glance, a touch, can lift me high,
A word, a sigh, can make me sigh.

To earn my trust, patience is key,
A gentle touch, a willingness to see,
Effort invested to keep me near,
In understanding, love shall appear.

I sense the shifts in your energy's flow,
The tremble in your voice, the ebb and glow,
Through every trial, thick or thin,
I'll stand beside you, heart within.

For I know the power of the small,
How they can lift us, catch us when we fall,
In details, in nuances, I find my guide,
In the depths of empathy, we'll abide.

The Key To Me

In travels wide, my soul took flight,
Unknowingly, in your presence alight,
As you roamed afar, my essence clung,
Leaving me in longing, songs unsung.

In absence felt, a vacant space,
My soul adrift, without a trace,
Yet all along, it dwelled with you,
A silent bond, profound and true.

Only when I journeyed near,
Did I sense my soul draw near,
In your embrace, it found its home,
A reunion sweet, no more to roam.

The Absence Of My Soul

In your eyes, love's ember burned bright,
A flame that danced in the depths of night,
But in that gaze, a truth revealed,
A love once cherished now concealed.

Through your eyes, I felt the glow,
A warmth that wrapped around me so,
Yet in their depths, a silent shift,
Love's fading spark, a painful rift.

It was in your eyes, the change I saw,
A love once fierce, now lost its awe,
Though it pains me so to see it clear,
In your eyes, love's absence seared.

The Way You Look At Me

In the depths of yearning, a fervent plea,
To hold you close, to make you mine, decree,
I longed to brand your name upon my soul,
To carve it deep, to make you whole.

Across my heart, your name to spread,
A testament to the love we've led,
Into my flesh, your name to etch,
A pledge of love, no break, no stretch.

To shield you from the world's cruel stare,
To bear your burdens, your scars to share,
In claiming you, I sought to impart,
A love so fierce, to mend your heart.
To always be here even if apart.

H o w   I   W a n t   Y o u

In the silence of my fears, I sought to dwell,
To sit amidst my suffering's somber swell.
With fears that gnawed, relentless, and unkind,
I grappled with a truth that weighed my mind.

Accepting that love, perhaps, was not for me,
Who gave it freely, yet alone I'd be.
For those who crafted it for others' grace,
Found solace in the warmth of love's embrace.

In solitude, I faced the depth of pain,
Wallowing in shadows, where doubts reign.
But in the depths, a flicker softly gleamed, A
gentle touch can dry the bitter tears.

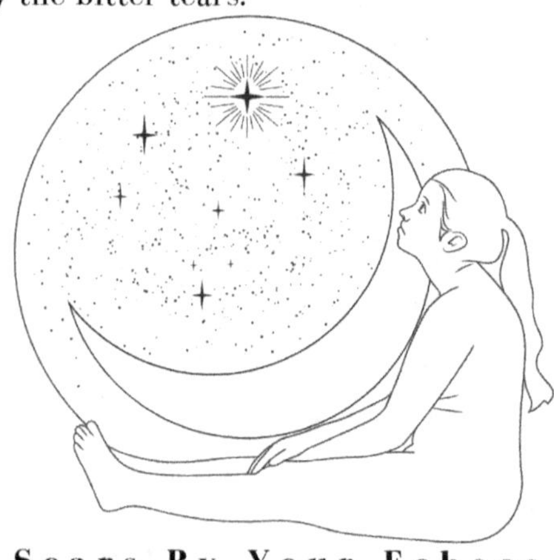

S c a r s   B y   Y o u r   E c h o e s

In the quiet of night, your voice once sweet,
Bid farewell with a silence, cold and discreet.
No more songs to lull me to rest,
Left alone in the darkness, my heart's unrest.

With each passing hour, sleep eludes,
As memories of your absence intrude.
The echo of your words, now lost in the night,
Leaves me wide-eyed, in solitude's plight.

Without your whispered "night night" to hear,
I lay awake, consumed by fear.
For in your absence, dreams have fled,
Left behind in a restless bed.

No longer do I find solace in sleep,
In this void, your absence runs deep.
With each silent night, the ache grows steep,
As I lie awake, in a world so bleak.

Silent Nights, Sleepless Eyes

In the shadowed depths of pain's embrace,
Your kiss, a light, a saving grace.
You sensed my need, my silent plea,
And with your touch, you set me free.

"I can't bear it," I whispered, weak,
But your love, a language, showed me peace.
"Kiss me," you urged, soft and clear,
And in that moment, all doubt disappeared.

With trembling lips, I met your own,
A silent promise, in love's tone.
"I kissed you, I kissed you," echoes through,
A testament to love, pure and true.

Kiss Me

In the silent chambers where anguish dwells,
"It didn't hurt," whispered amidst the swells.
For 'hurt' is but a frail façade,
Beside the tempest that left her raw and flawed.

Destroyed, shattered, and butcher,
Her spirit endured the relentless uproar.
Desecrated dreams in the midnight's pall,
Annihilated trust, yet remained the call.

No mere hurt, but a tempestuous surge,
Demolishing illusions, truth did emerge.
Shattered fragments of a once whole soul,
Yet from the abyss, resilience stole.

So in the stillness of the darkest night.
"It didn't hurt," echoed amidst the blight.

It Didn't Hurt

In absence, I convince myself I'll cope,
Yet in her embrace, I find my hope.
Nestled in the nape of her neck so dear,
Lies a refuge I crave when she's not near.

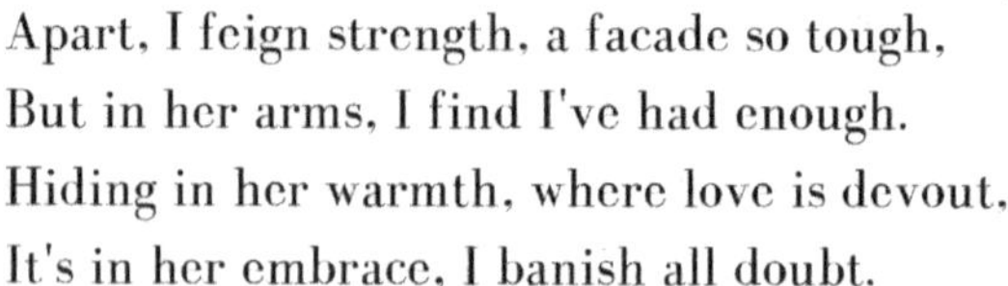

Apart, I feign strength, a facade so tough,
But in her arms, I find I've had enough.
Hiding in her warmth, where love is devout,
It's in her embrace, I banish all doubt.

So every time we part, I bid goodbye,
Yet in her tender hold, I can't deny,
The solace found in the nape of her neck,
A sanctuary I yearn for, a love to beck.

In Your Neck

Love, a delicate dance of trust and sway,
Granting power, come what may.
To entrust one's heart, a fragile art,
Believing they'll guard it, never tear it apart.

In vulnerability's grip, we surrender our might,
Hoping they'll cherish, not incite.
For in love's embrace, we find our truth,
A bond that withstands the test of youth.

So we give freely, with hearts aglow,
Trusting they'll handle it with care, not woe.
For in the gamble of love's tender quest,
Lies the essence of faith, at its behest.

What Is Love

In the mirror's gaze, beauty shines bright,
Yet within, shadows lurk, a constant fight.
A bitter taste, a rotting core,
Unveiling depths unseen before.

Pushed to the brink, claws may extend,
Yet tears at beauty, at love, they blend.
For in the spaces between, a soul does yearn,
Aching for solace, a chance to discern.

Out of character, actions replay,
Thoughts cling tight, night and day.
Not cruel, just lost in the storm,
Seeking refuge from emotions, forlorn.

Beneath anger's veil, sadness lies,
A defense mechanism in disguise.
Biting back tears, until the light,
Tilts the balance, breaking through the night.

Struggling to reveal the softness within,
A quest for acceptance, a battle to win.
To prove resilience in the face of strife,
That despite it all, there's still life.

The Mirror

In the tapestry of fate, threads intertwine,
Souls drawn together, by design divine.
Destiny's hand, guiding each course,
Connections forged with an unseen force.

No meeting by chance, in life's grand scheme,
Each encounter a part of a cosmic dream.
Paths converge, hearts align,
In the dance of existence, by a sacred sign.

From fleeting glances to embraces tight,
Every meeting ignites a spark, a light.
For souls entwined, bound by a cosmic pact,
Each encounter a testament to an eternal fact.

Our Threaded Souls

Choose a partner whose commitment is true,
A Lilly that's right, just for you.
Who cherishes you each day, through and through.
Not just when the mood is right, but always near,
A steadfast presence, calming every fear.

In the ebb and flow of life's changing tide,
Find solace in a love that won't hide.
For in the choice to be by your side,
Lies the essence of a love that can't be denied.

Everyday Choice

In the realm where souls entwine,
A chance to make your world all mine.
But in the depths of my kind of love,
Beware, for I can be a tempest from above.

A handful, yes, with passions ablaze,
You might find yourself lost in the maze.
Overwhelmed by the depth of my care,
So pause and consider, if you dare.

For when you take my hand and agree,
To journey with me, wild and free,
Know this: it'll be unlike any before,
A love that leaves you craving more.

So, before you embrace what I offer anew,
Understand, it'll be an adventure true.
For my love, a whirlwind, a roaring sea,
An experience you'll cherish eternally.

A Maze Of Me

In the echo of doubt, you may find,
A whisper that tells you you're hard to bind.
But remember, dear heart, it's not your fault,
For those who failed to love you, their own halt.

Their inability to cherish your light,
Reflects the void within, not your might.
Don't let their shadows dim your glow,
For you're worthy of love, this you must know.

It's not your burden to bear their lack,
Their shortcomings, an echo from the past.
So stand tall, let your worth shine through,
For you're deserving of love, pure and true.

You Are Lovable

In the fire of your love, I find my flame,
Igniting passions, ambitions, the same.
You inspire me to chase my dreams,
To reach for the stars, to sail uncharted streams.

With you by my side, I feel I can soar,
Breaking barriers, unlocking each door.
You make me strive to be my best,
With your love as my compass, guiding my quest.

Every day with you, I see the light,
A beacon of hope, burning bright.
In your embrace, I find my truth,
A love so pure, so sweet, so youth.

You're the reason I want to grow and evolve,
To reach new heights, to problem-solve.
For in your love, I find my strength anew.

Days With You

In the tender glow of twilight's embrace,
Amidst our haven, our sacred space.
With moonbeams casting shadows on the floor,
We'll dance in the kitchen, forevermore.

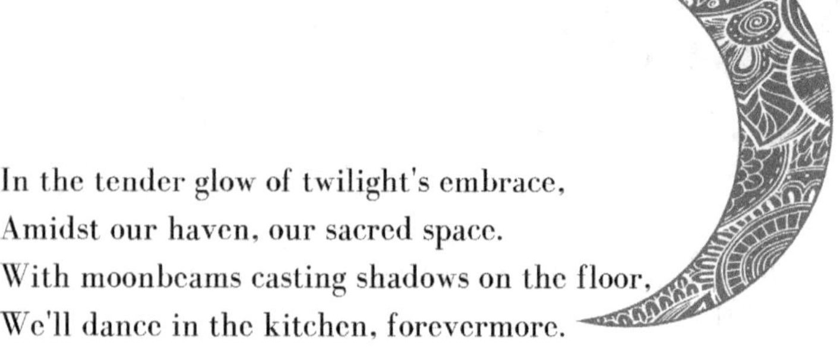

Wrapped in the warmth of love's gentle touch,
I'll hold you close, I'll cherish you much.
No passing years could dim our flame,
For our love, an eternal refrain.

Let them whisper we're fools, too young to see,
Yet in our hearts, we know what will be.
With every kiss, a symphony of grace,
I'll yearn for your lips, in this endless embrace.

You're my sanctuary, my solace, my home,
In your arms, all fears are overthrown.
No soul compares to the beauty you impart,
A masterpiece of love, a work of art.

So let's waltz in the moonlight, hand in hand,
In this eternal dance, together we'll stand.
For I vow to spend eternity,
Falling in love with you, endlessly.

Moonlight Dance

In the sacred space of vulnerability's embrace,
She poured out her heart, finding solace in the chase.
Opening up, like petals to the sun's warm light,
Confronting the shadows she once kept out of sight.

"I crave love," she confessed, voice trembling but clear,
"It's what I long for, yet I always fear."
She hesitated, unsure if she should reveal more,
But she pressed on, her truth she couldn't ignore.

"Im not worth it," she admitted, with a sigh,
A vulnerability laid bare, beneath the sky.
And then came the words, like a gentle embrace,
"But you are worthy," spoken with unwavering grace.

As if it were a truth etched in stone,
"You're everything to me," she said, not alone.
Her words a balm to the wounds deep inside,
A reminder of worth, where doubts may reside.

For in that moment, in the sharing of pain,
A bond was forged, a connection to sustain.
And though the journey ahead may be tough,
With love and support, they'll weather the rough.

You Are Worthy

No more will I plead my case,
No more will I seek solace in grace.
If fault is all you choose to see,
Then so be it, I'll let it be.

No more explanations, no more tears,
No more facing judgment's fears.
I refuse to beg for understanding,
In this silence, I find my standing.

Things I was afraid to hear,
You admitted to me all to near.
I searched your eyes, looking for a lie
But all I found were severed ties.

Twisted Lies

In moments bright, her love does shine,
When joy's embrace makes her divine.
Yet when I fracture, like grains of sand,
She lets me go, alone I stand.

When smiles adorn my face so fair,
Her angelic touch, beyond compare.
But shattered dreams, and heartache sore,
Left to wander, on distant shore.

She loves me whole, in blissful flight,
Yet when I fall, she takes her flight.
Alone amidst the shards, I see,
Her love's conditionality.

Conditional Love

Lost in the labyrinth of life's design,
A path unclear, a wandering mind.
Yet in the depths of uncertainty's hold,
Discovery awaits, a story untold.

For in the wilderness of the unknown,
Opportunity whispers, seeds are sown.
Amidst confusion's tangled vines,
Clarity emerges, a beacon shines.

So fear not the journey, though twists may unwind,
For being lost can lead to treasures to find.
In the unraveling maze, new paths are bound,
Lost souls find solace, and wisdom is found.

Lost Souls

Under the weight of expectations, I crumbled,
Striving to fit into a mold, so perfectly humbled.
Every fragment of self, shattered and strained,
In pursuit of a fleeting glance, love feigned.

I sacrificed my essence, lost in her gaze,
A heroin rush, fleeting moments ablaze.
Yet as I overdosed on her fleeting affection,
I realized the cost, a soul's disconnection.

In the quest to be the girl she desired,
I lost myself, consumed by the fire.

To Be The Perfect Girl

In a world where love's scarce, I sought to be craved,
To feel desired, in ways unexplained.
I was wanted, yes, in fleeting embrace,
But love's tender touch, I couldn't trace.

Never bathed in love's gentle light,
Yet in being wanted, found some respite.
A hunger fulfilled, but soul still yearned,
For love's deeper bond, yet to be earned.

In the realm of desires, I found my place,
But the ache for true love, left its trace.
Yearning for more than mere attraction,
In the depths of the heart, seeking satisfaction.

Never Loved

In the moments shared, a hunger stirred,
Desire ignited, every touch conferred.
Pulling her close, soft and warm,
Feeling alive, in love's sweet storm.

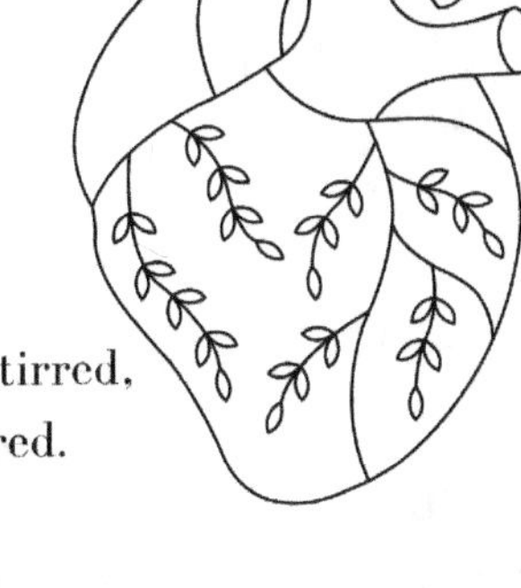

Carrying her to bed, a tender embrace,
A newfound joy, a lover's grace.
Every minute with her, a precious treasure,
Her essence consumed, a love to measure.

Yet hunger remained, an insatiable thirst,
For her, I yearned, a love immersed.
Breathing her in, tasting her sweet embrace,
But still craving more, in love's relentless chase.

How to satisfy this hunger, love's endless plea?
In the depths of passion, finding unity.
For in loving her, I find my release,
In her arms, my hunger finds its peace.

This Insatiable Love

Your words paint a picture of pure affection,
In your embrace, finding love's perfection.
"Baby" whispers sweet, a tender name,
In your arms, I find solace, free from shame.

Together, we weave a tapestry of bliss,
Each moment shared, a cherished kiss.
You're my safe harbor, my guiding light,
In your presence, everything feels right.

Wrapped in your love, I find my place,
In your arms, a sacred embrace.
You're not just mine, but my soul's delight,
Forever entwined, in love's endless flight.

B a b y

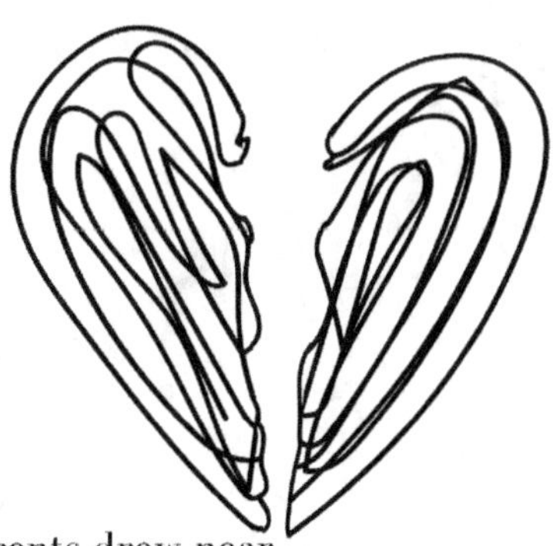

In the hush of dusk, as my parents drew near,
Guilt swirled like mist, in the atmosphere.
Forced apart by their timely return,
Our love, a candle's flame, destined to burn.

I mourn the sweet moments we could not share,
As they arrived, casting shadows of despair.
With heavy heart, I watched you depart,
Feeling the weight of guilt tear me apart.

I never wanted you to leave, not this way,
But their presence dictated our disarray.
My heart aches with the burden I bear,
For driving you away, in silent despair.

In the echo of parting, a whispered plea,
For one more moment, just you and me.
Yet amidst the anguish, one truth rings clear,
In the depths of my guilt, my love for you, dear.

The Guilt Of You

Your words weave a tapestry of devotion rare,
A love beyond casual, a bond we share.
Cooking your favorite meal, crafting jewelry with care,
Love letters penned, whispers of love in the air.

Nails painted the color of your eyes so bright,
In your embrace, finding solace each night.
Playing with your hair till sleep claims its due,
Sharing clothes, melding into one, me and you.

Listening to your music, every note so sweet,
Capturing moments, memories to keep.
Hand in hand, through life's ebb and flow,
Every detail of your day, I long to know.

Reminding you, endlessly, of my love so true,
In every heartbeat, I find you anew.
For in these simple gestures, love's story we tell,
Bound together, in a love deeper than words can spell.

Bound Together

In the depths of my being, a fire burns bright,
Adoring you, craving you, in love's pure light.
Obsessed, perhaps, in the healthiest way,
For you're the stardust that lights up my day.

The universe whispered, you're made of starlight,
A truth I embrace, in love's endless flight.
Magical, wondrous, when you enter the room,
Each wave whispers your name, in love's sweet perfume.

The sun rises, just to light up your face,
The moon graces us, with its gentle embrace.
I don't just like you, it's deeper than that,
A love that transcends, in moments so fat.

Yet words fail me, in capturing this love so grand,
No alphabet's perfect, to express where we stand.
But in the touch of your hand, the sound of your voice,
My soul ignites, in love's timeless rejoice.

So if words falter, know it's not in vain,
For my love for you, forever will reign.
In silence, in whispers, our love will endure,
For in loving you deeply, my soul finds its cure.

Y o u,   Y o u

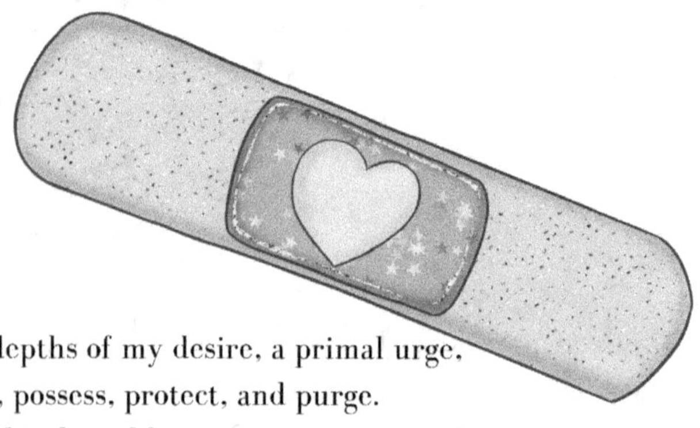

In the depths of my desire, a primal urge,
To own, possess, protect, and purge.
I wanted to brand her name upon my soul,
To shield her from darkness, to make her whole.

To carve her name into my flesh so deep,
So she wouldn't feel alone in scars that creep.
I longed to intertwine our fates as one,
To bear her burdens until the battle's won.

But in my longing, I realize the truth,
Love's not about possession or eternal youth.
It's about lifting her up, setting her free,
Embracing her scars, with empathy.

So instead of branding, I offer my hand,
To walk beside her, through shifting sand.
Together we'll conquer, whatever may be,
For her scars and mine, make us truly free.

Your Scars

In the rawness of my anguish, I poured out my soul,
Bearing the scars of betrayal, beyond my control.
"You broke me," the words echoed, stark and true,
Bleeding into the pain I'd endured, through and through.

"You fucked me up, tearing at me"
the pain searing deep inside,
Yet you return, each time, despite the tears of blood I
cried.
Why, oh why, do you persist in this cruel game?
Why do you continue to fan the flames of my shame?

Her response, a dagger, piercing through the air,
The most honest words, laid bare and rare.
"You let me," she whispered, a truth hard to bear,
A mirror reflecting my own despair.

In that moment of truth, terror gripped my heart,
For in letting her in, I played my part.
Bur oh how I'd play it again and again,
for in this game, she loves me so.

Is It Betrayal

My love for you runs deep,
A whispered symphony, secrets to keep.
A million times, I could have confessed,
Yet I yearned for you to truly digest.

To fathom its essence, its celestial glow,
To embody its essence, in every ebb and flow.
And if given the chance, I'd echo it true,
A thousand and two, just for you.

Still, my affection for you remains,
A sweet refrain, amid life's refrains.
For what it's worth, I comprehend,
Beyond the surface, where hearts transcend.

The ramifications of knowing you,
Unleashed a love, wild and true.
Unyielding, unmatched, it stands tall,
A flame untamed, destined to enthral.

Love unbound, in its purest form,
Infinite as the cosmos, weathering storm.
Like a rose in bloom, with thorns unseen,
Its beauty profound, in every scene.

So I'll continue to love, with each heartbeat,
In your garden of love, my soul finds its seat.
For even amidst thorns, love finds its way,
In your embrace, forever to stay.

You Still

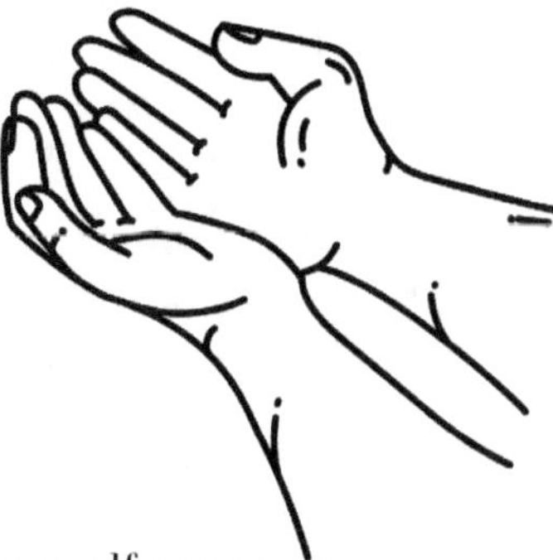

In the silence of solitude, I find myself once more,
Locked in the bathroom, the sink's gentle roar.
Drowning out the echoes of pain, so deep,
Afraid to reach out, to awaken from sleep.

I claimed I was healing, moving towards the light,
Yet here I am, lost in the shadows of night.
Curled up in my bed, blankets clenched tight,
Muffling my cries, in the darkness of night.

"I'm okay," I whispered, a facade so frail,
But the truth remains, a bitter, harsh tale.
Frozen in time, unable to break free,
From the chains of hurt, that bind me.

I never was healing, as I claimed to be,
Trapped in the past, unable to see.
But amidst the darkness, a glimmer of hope,
A light in the distance, a way to cope.

For healing begins with acknowledging the pain,
Taking a step forward, despite the strain.
Though the journey is long, and the path unclear,
I'll find my way, away from fear.

My Plea

In the stillness of her gaze, a fervent vow,
"You could lay waste to planets, this I avow.
Yet even amidst the ruins, I'd gladly stray,
If by your side, I could humbly stay."

Her words, a tempest, stirring my soul,
With every syllable, her love took its toll.
My heart trembled, with the weight they bore,
A devotion profound, forevermore.

"If that's love," she whispered, his tone sincere,
"Then yes, I love you," her confession clear.
"I can't help but love you," she softly sighed,
A truth unyielding, her heart open wide.

In her unwavering devotion, I found my grace,
A love so fierce, it lit up every space.
For in her arms, I found my sanctuary,
Amidst the chaos, a beacon, necessary.

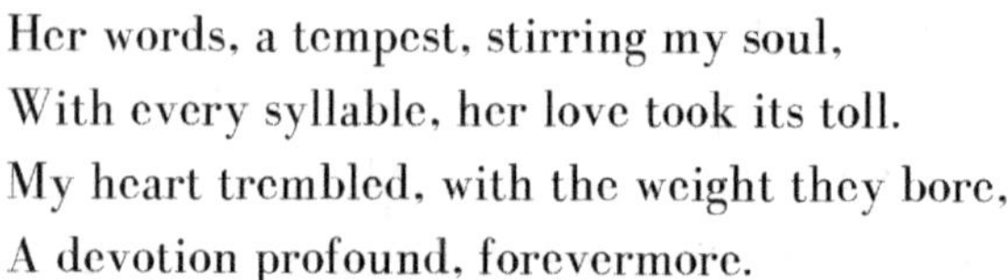

How I Love You

I longed for tender words, a gentle plea,
"Stay soft," I hoped, "its perfectly made for you."
But instead, you urged me to harden, to toughen my core,
To become a rock, not a flower anymore.

Your words pierced deep, a dagger to my soul,
Shattering my hopes, leaving me feeling whole.
For in your rejection, I lost a piece of me,
Yearning for the softness, that once set me free.

I wanted to bloom, to embrace my fragility,
But your insistence on hardness, clouded my ability.
It shattered my dreams, left me feeling alone,
Longing for acceptance, in a heart turned to stone.

Yet even amidst the rubble, I'll find my way,
Reclaiming my softness, come what may.
For in embracing vulnerability, I'll find my power,
No longer defined by your desire to tower.

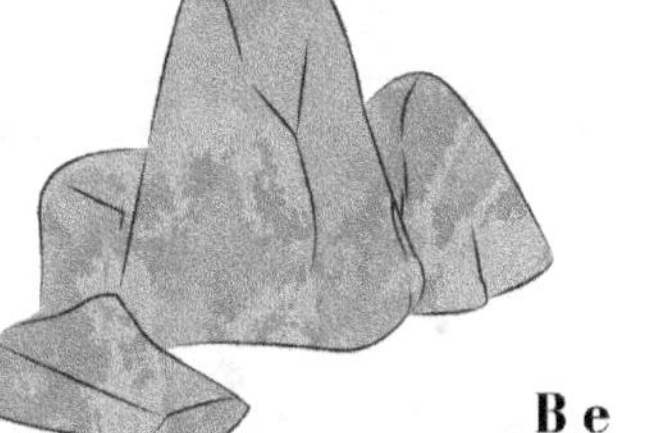

Be A Rock, Not A Flower

Her nose meets mine, her lips on mine, a surge of electricity,
My breath halts, caught in this moment's serenity.
"I love you," she murmurs, a symphony of affection,
Each word, a gentle touch, a divine connection.

With closed eyes, I feel the shift within,
Her words, like gentle waves, washing away sin.
Creating something new, within my core,
I swallow hard, feeling love's allure.

Fire dances in my mind, under her gaze,
Every word, every touch, sets my soul ablaze.
"I love you," I admit,
As her lips trace my jawline, a gentle hit.

Her love, a warmth coursing through my veins,
Her whispers, like echoes in eternal refrains.
For a fleeting moment, I'm lost in reverie,
Where love's embrace becomes my reality.

I Love You

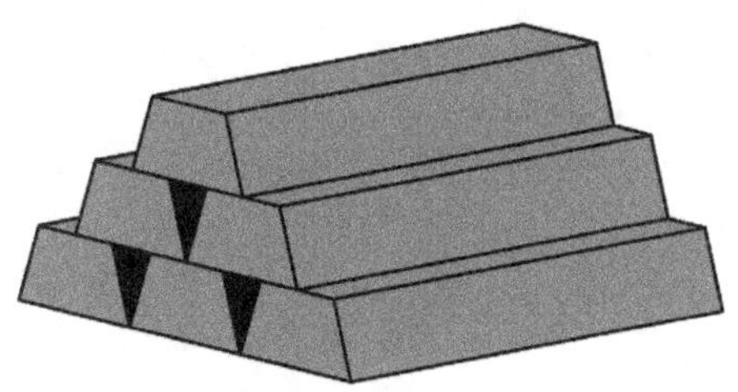

In a world bathed in silver hue,
You shine like gold, bright and true.
Amongst the shadows, you stand bold,
A beacon of light, a treasure to behold.

With every step, you grace the earth,
A radiant presence of immeasurable worth.
In your essence, love's story is told,
If the rest of the world was silver, then you were gold.

Your warmth, a touch that soothes the soul,
In your embrace, broken hearts find their role.
In a world of fleeting moments, you unfold,
A timeless beauty, a love untold.

So let the world gleam in silver's glow,
For in your presence, love's true colors show.
In a realm where treasures are bought and sold,
If the rest of the world was silver, then you were gold.

You're Gold

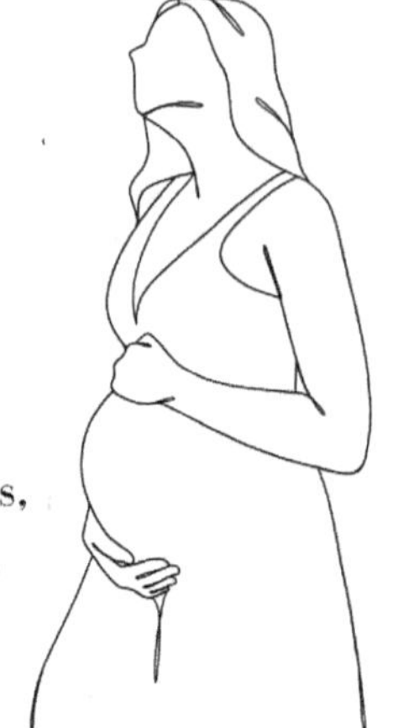

In your dreams, you speak of future days,
Of children's laughter, in a home ablaze.
Yet I know, I can't bear them for you,
The ache in my heart, a love so true.

To imagine you with another, to fulfill that dream,
Is a dagger to my soul, a silent scream.
The thought of you with someone new,
Breaks me, shatters me, through and through.

My love for children, once vibrant and clear,
Now fades into the shadows, in the absence of you near.
To wallow in this emptiness, this void,
Is to dwell in the pain, with hope destroyed.

Yet amidst the sorrow, a flicker of light,
A glimmer of hope, in the depths of night.
For love's path is winding, its course unknown,
Perhaps in time, seeds of hope will be sown.

But for now, I mourn the loss of what could be,
In the absence of you, in the absence of we.

K i d s   Y o u   E a s i l y   S p e a k   O f

In the silence of your absence, I'm left to wonder why,
You shut me out, leaving me to cry.
Busy signals and unanswered calls,
Each rejection, another brick in love's walls.

I love you, I scream into the void,
But your indifference leaves me destroyed.
Why won't you see me, why won't you care?
In your absence, love becomes despair.

If it were me, I'd run to your side,
Not waste a moment, not let love hide.
I'd answer every call, reply to every text,
But your silence leaves me feeling perplexed.

With each ignored message, I fade away,
Lost in the shadows of love's disarray.
Don't you see, don't you understand?
Your indifference, like quicksand.

It's making me fade, this silence so loud,
In the absence of love, I'm left feeling cowed.
But still, I cling to hope, in love's embrace,
Praying for a glimpse of your face.

User Busy

"Do you love me?" echoes in the night,
A question born of doubt, a flickering light.
"Do you love me, or just want me so?"
In the depths of uncertainty, we quietly grow.

"Are you bored?" whispers the wind,
A fear that lingers, where doubts begin.
"Am I merely for your entertainment?"
In the shadows of doubt, we seek containment.

Questions unanswered, linger in the air,
As we grapple with doubts, and the weight we bear.
But amidst the uncertainty, a truth remains,
Love's whispers endure, through joys and pains.

For love transcends the doubts that we see,
It's found in moments, shared tenderly.
So let's embrace the uncertainty, and fears that bind,
For in love's embrace, true solace we find.

Questions You Never Answered

In the quiet of night, in the depths of my soul,
Even after everything, it's still you, I behold.
The ache of longing, a bittersweet hue,
For it's still you, my heart yearns to pursue.

Through trials and tribulations, through joys and pain,
It's your presence I seek, again and again.
For amidst the chaos, in love's enduring view,
It's still you, my heart holds onto.

The echoes of your laughter, the touch of your hand,
In every corner of my being, your presence stands.
So sad, yet so true, in all that I do,
It's still you, my love, I continue to pursue.

Yearning For You

You broke me, shattered my heart in two,
Yet I still hold you as the greatest, it's true.
In the wreckage of love, amidst the debris,
I find solace in the truth that I loved you deeply.

Through tears and pain, through the darkest night,
Your memory shines, a beacon of light.
For in loving you, I found my soul's refrain,
Even as I nurse the wounds of love's disdain.

So I hold onto the memories, both bitter and sweet,
For they're proof of a love that was once complete.
Though you broke me, tore me apart at the seams,
In my heart, you'll always be the stuff of dreams.

True, True

In the depths of despair, where pain resides,
It hurts to be broken, where love abides.
A heart shattered, torn apart at the seams,
Yet love remains, haunting our dreams.

The ache of betrayal, the sting of deceit,
Yet love's flame flickers, refusing defeat,
To love the one who caused such sorrow,
Is a burden to bear, come each tomorrow.

Through tears and anguish, we carry the weight,
Knowing love endures, despite our fate.
In the silence of heartache, love finds its voice,
Aching and longing, yet still our choice.

For love knows no bounds, no reason or rhyme,
It persists through the pain, through the test of time.
So we hold onto love, despite the strain,
In the midst of brokenness, it still remains.

In The Brokenness

In every word, a whisper of devotion,
Expressions of love, in heartfelt motion.
"To the grocery store," a tender query,
"Need anything?" Love's gentle theory.

"Open your door," a gift unfurled,
A token of affection, in this world.
"Did you reach home safe?" A heartfelt plea,
A reminder of love's constancy.

"I'm proud of you," a celestial hymn,
A melody of support, through life's whim.
"Let's journey together," a shared flight,
In the depths of love's resplendent light.

"I'll stand by your side," a vow profound,
Through valleys low, and peaks renowned.
"I'll prepare this time," a culinary feat,
Nourishing body and soul, love replete.

"How do you fare, truly?" A question deep,
Inviting truth, in love's endless sweep.
"I hold an extra ticket," a gesture grand,
In unity and harmony, hand in hand.

"May fortune favor you," a whispered prayer,
Encouragement woven, through love's air.
"How may I assist?" A gentle plea,
In love's embrace, forever free.

"Shall we share this moment?" A blissful delight,
In each other's company, worlds unite.
"I shall collect you," a pledge refined,
In love's embrace, intertwined.

"Speak to me of your day," a gentle plea,
In the sanctuary of love's decree.
"Remember our shared tales," a journey divine,
In memories cherished, love entwined.

"At eight, prepare for a surprise," a whispered tale,
Anticipation dances, love's veiled veil.
"Together, let us navigate," a united stand,
In love's sanctuary, hand in hand.

"In your absence, life's void looms," a heartfelt plea,
In your presence, love's symphony.
Each message, a testament, to love's eternal hue,
In every breath, I cherish you.

My Language Of Love

Once, just a kiss, a whisper of desire,
Could we rewind, extinguish passion's fire?
Perhaps we could, if we tread with care,
But what if longing lingers in the air?

Twice embraced, in moments of bliss,
Sleeping close, caught in love's sweet abyss.
Making memories, hearts beating as one,
Can we turn back now that it's begun?

Exhausted from farewells, from love's cruel game,
Why must we extinguish what ignites the flame?
Why sever ties, forever to part,
When love still beats within each heart?

Why deny the truth that we both know,
Why suppress the feelings that continue to grow?
Let's acknowledge our love, let passion begin,
And embrace the journey that lies within.

Let 's Give In

ACKNOWLEDGEMENTS

In the journey of crafting this collection, there are countless individuals whose support and presence have illuminated my path.

To Lola, whose essence infuses every word, every line, and every verse of this book, I extend my deepest gratitude.

Lola, you are the gravity that keeps me grounded, the melody that colours my days, and the unwavering force that guides me through life's labyrinth. Our journey together has been a whirlwind of emotions, filled with peaks and valleys, yet your presence remains the constant north star that guides my soul. Through the highs and lows, your unwavering love and companionship have been my guiding light. You entered my life and effortlessly turned it on its head, or perhaps it was I who found myself ensnared in the beautiful chaos of yours. With each passing moment, you prove to be more than everything I ever dreamed of, and I find myself unable to imagine a single day without your radiant presence. You are more than my everything; you are the very essence of my existence. Not a day passes without your radiant presence, not a moment unfurls without your touch upon my soul. This book is not merely a collection of words, but a testament to the profound love and connection we share.

Lola, I offer this labour of love to you, alongside every heartbeat, every whispered promise, and every breathless moment we've shared. With boundless affection and immeasurable gratitude, I dedicate this book to you, my beloved, and offer this humble testament of my affection. I love you my Lilly. Always and forever.